A PERSONAL PRAYER BOOK

PERSONAL PRAYERS FOR WOMEN

Brief prayers particularly for
women to help in praying each
day

GRACE SIMPSON

DIMENSIONS
FOR LIVING
NASHVILLE

PERSONAL PRAYERS FOR WOMEN

This book is printed on recycled, acid-free, elemental-chlorine–free paper.

Library of Congress Cataloging-in-Publication Data

Personal prayers for women : brief prayers : particularly for women
in praying each day / [edited by] Grace Simpson.
    p. cm. — (A personal prayer book)
    ISBN 0-687-05254-8 (alk. paper)
    1. Prayers. 2. Women—Prayer-books and devotions—English.
I. Simpson, Grace, 1940- II. Series.

BV283.W6 P47 2002
242'.843—dc21

                                                    2001056182

Scripture quotations are from the New Revised Standard Version of
the Bible, copyright © 1989 by the Division of Christian Education
of the National Council of the Churches of Christ in the U.S.A.

04 05 06 07 08 09 10 11–10 9 8 7 6 5 4

A GOD OF WISDOM

Lord, I thank you that you are a God who is with me at every turn; you never get tired of being with me. But you're not a clinging God. I praise your wisdom that allows me to be an individual; that gives me the freedom to make choices and so learn and develop as a person. And when, in my freedom, I make mistakes, again, you're always there to help mop up and get me on my feet again.

Forgive me for those times when I act as though you don't even exist; while, in actual fact, your wisdom, love, and care are in operation for me every second of my life. As, indeed, they are for all your children and for all your creation.

Fill my heart and mind and mouth with praise for such greatness and with thanks that you stoop to bless me with it. Amen.

Summer Days

Lord, the crickets and cicadas are hard at it, chirping and singing their little hearts out; simply, I guess, from the sheer joy of being alive on a warm, sunny day.

I know how they feel. Thank you for these summer days that throb with life, that pulsate with the joy of living. They make me feel good; maybe partly because, in all their vibrancy, they remind me of the quality of life I share with you—life that's vibrant, rich, and pulsating because it comes from you, the one who *is* life.

I praise you, Jesus, you who are the Life. Thank you for giving me *life in all its fullness. Amen.*

Stillness

Dear Lord, my life can get so cluttered up with the many little things I have to attend to. A day can be nothing more for me than a darting here and there from morning to night.

Help me not to feel guilty for standing still or sitting quietly now and then. At such times let me absorb the stillness and the space around me, unpunctuated by my flurried movements. And then, impart some of that stillness into my being so that it becomes absorbed into my movements, giving them greater direction, and saving them from a busyness that becomes its own end.

Grant that each day I carry within me that best of all stillnesses—your peace—so that there is a stability underlying my days, however busy they may be. Amen.

THE SWEETNESS OF JESUS

God, the garbage can smelled terrible when I opened it this morning! It must have been the remnants of Monday's fish dinner. I know garbage cans aren't meant to smell like a rose garden, but that smell this morning was beyond the pale.

I wonder, God, whether you wrinkle your nose in distaste as the horrible stench of my pride and self-centeredness and apathy wafts heavenward. You have to put up with an awful lot, don't you? I'm sorry.

I'm also very thankful that the sweet perfume of Jesus' goodness pleases you so much—because I'm banking on his sweetness to obliterate my foulness. Amen.

THE HELPER

Don't fall over, Lord; we've cleaned the windows. With the two of us at it, my husband doing the outside and me the inside, we had the whole house done by lunchtime. If I'd known it was going to be such a breeze with his help, I'd have tackled it much sooner—I think.

Thanks, Lord, that marriage gives one the chance to share the yucky jobs.

And thank you that you're with me whenever I have to tackle something in life that I'd rather not. I don't know that your presence always makes it a breeze, but it sure helps. Amen.

Save me from misery

What gives me the right, God, to be especially miserable, as if I were someone special?

Thanks for hitting me over the head today with a fresh realization of the fact that everyone else out there has problems and difficulties too. I am, after all, no different from others. And if so many of them can get up and get on with their lives instead of standing around moping and wringing their hands in despair, then so can I.

In fact, I can go one better: I can face each day with the knowledge that you are with me as I begin that day and as I go through it.

Save me, God, from my miserable self! Amen.

Routine Jobs

God, I've just come home from doing the shopping, and going to the bank and the library, and filling up the car with gas—all the usual once-a-week jobs. They probably make up my least enjoyable activities for the week (except for the library visit). I particularly dislike having to put away all the supermarket stuff once it's out of the car and inside the house.

And yet I know that it's this week-by-week sort of activity that helps bring a sense of stability and security into my life—especially at those times when everything else in my world is falling apart.

Thank you, God, for the blessing that comes with performing routine jobs. Amen.

A MOTHER'S WORRIES

Dear God, I'm worried sick about my son. I wonder how he's ever going to get through the year; his study workload is tremendous. And then he's got to find somewhere to live—thank you that at least his friend will put him up for the time being. And, without a car, he could be in all sorts of difficulties when it comes to getting around for his work study.

Rob is your child too, isn't he? He became your child at his rebirth in his baptism. Well—I'm asking you to be a dad now to this child of yours. Care for him: direct him, protect him, give him special strength as he needs it; in fact, be there for him in all his needs as the perfect dad that you are. I know that you have a good plan for my boy's life, so I guess if I keep handing him over to you in my prayers, I can relax knowing he's in the best of hands; and that, because of this, everything will turn out all right.

I feel much better now. Thank you! Amen.

THANKS FOR A FRIEND

God, thank you for my best friend and her gentle nature. When I'm in her home I feel her gentleness and quietness washing over me, smoothing down my rough edges. And then, for a day or two, my abrasiveness and abruptness are not quite so abrasive and abrupt.

Thank you for a friend who gives me this special blessing.

It's wonderful, Lord, how you arrange things in our lives so that we are given, through others, those things that we ourselves lack and need. Amen.

A GOOD DAY

Dear Lord, may today be a good day for me and mine—whether it's good because things go well for us, or whether because, in our troubles, we are brought closer to you.

How I love those days when all is sunshine and satisfaction! They're good days, Lord, and I thank you for them.

But teach us to see that our difficult days are also good days because they are opportunities for us to grow in our relationship with you. Thank you that our troubles lead us to your word, so that we can be blessed by the truth of all your promises there to care for us. Thank you that our difficulties lead us to experience all over again the blessing that comes through trusting you. And thank you for the new insights we gain into your greatness as we see it at work, helping us in our hard times. What better thing can there be for us in life than to be brought closer to you, the one who is goodness?

Thank you for this day, Lord. It is truly a good day—whatever happens. Amen.

Belonging

Lord, I'm feeling a bit blue today in my single-ness. Maybe I shouldn't have gone to the tennis picnic. Everywhere I looked there seemed to be a group of mom, dad, and the kids. Well, nearly everywhere. It's true, we had our single parents; but they still had their children.

People were kind and friendly to me. And why not? They're my friends. But I couldn't help feeling my difference from everyone else. They all belonged to someone, and I didn't.

But that's not true, is it? I do belong to someone. I belong to you, and you're the greatest companion anyone could have. You love me, you care for me, you're always there when I particularly need you. It's just that I need the Holy Spirit to remind me of this every now and then.

Jesus, you came to earth to give me a rich, full life. Lead on; I'm right behind you! Amen.

Happy Memories

Dear Lord, after all the tidying up and vacuuming I've done since the wedding, I still came across a piece of confetti today. (I wonder what that says about my housekeeping?)

It delighted my heart to see that little bright pink spot peeping out from beneath the piano, because it brought back to me all the happiness of the day our daughter got married.

Thank you, Lord, not just for the joy of that day of high celebration with dear ones, but also for answering a mother's prayer to give her daughter the right husband.

This is one grateful mom. Amen.

A PRAYER FOR HEALING

Dear God, you know why I'm coming to you now: I want your healing for my friend. I want it so badly that I feel like *insisting* you heal her! After all, if anyone can do it, you can: you're God.

But I guess it's just because you're God that I can't call the tune. That's for you to do because, as God, you know so much better than we humans.

I'll keep asking you to heal her because your word says to ask; and I do believe you can heal her. I believe also that your love will keep on flowing to her in a steady stream, whatever happens; and that it will bring with it all sorts of good things for her.

Give her the best now—whatever, in your wisdom, that happens to be. Amen.

Destructive moths

Wretched moths! I've just chased two of them in the kitchen and managed to squash only one. They play havoc with the pantry foods, and I live in dread of what they might do to our clothing.

Last week I found, on a pantry shelf, the most revolting-looking half-eaten packet of walnut pieces. The moths and their grubs had had a great time with them. And I also noticed recently that our old gray blankets are sporting a few extra holes. They're so ancient that's no great loss; perhaps our children can use them for camping one day. But I'll have to do something to protect my good blankets.

Thank you, Lord, that one day I'll be living in a place "where neither moth nor rust consumes." I'm looking forward to that! Not only will all the treasures of heaven be mine, but, what's more, they'll never be spoiled. Not by anything.

With that in mind, Lord, I guess I can put up with these moths a bit longer. Amen.

The Comforter

Lord, as I hear the groaning tones of the washing machine, I'm comforted. Dirty clothes must be washed, dried, ironed, folded, and put away. Life must go on, they say; and in the familiar smell and sounds of doing the washing, I'm beginning to see that this is true.

Perhaps, as I keep on going through the motions of everyday living, the ache and emptiness I carry inside me will eventually lessen.

These are those, Lord, who hurt as I do and yet have no chance to ease their pain in things familiar because the familiar has been torn away from them through war or natural disasters.

Holy Spirit—Comforter—be a comfort to them and me as only you are able to be. Amen.

As Children Grow Up

Lord God, help me not to over-identify with my children.

I love them deeply, but give me the wisdom to know when to involve myself in their problems and when to stand back far enough to let them do their own struggling, so that they can grow as individuals. Keep me from stunting their growth through an overly strong desire to protect them from life's hardships; their development can so easily be smothered and stifled by my well-meaning love for them.

Let my love for my children be the sort of love that frees them to be their own person, and—especially— to be the person you want them to be. Amen.

Changing Seasons

It's autumn now, God, and the days have a different flavor. The rich, full-bodied taste of summer has been replaced by the more delicate menu of paler, softer sunlight and cooler breezes.

Thank you for the different joys that the individual seasons bring us. I'm glad of all the times I'll be sharing with you as I see something to thank you for in this new season.

And I'm so glad that, from one season to the next, you *remain a constant joy! Amen.*

TRANSPLANTED

I should have done this years ago: transplanted this hydrangea from this fairly dark area to a sunnier spot. I hope it will now grow into a nicely rounded shape and produce more blooms. That will be a big improvement on the tall, leggy, sparsely producing plant it has been in the past.

Lord, if you want to place me somewhere where I can grow and be more productive for you, then go ahead. It's the least I can do after all you've done for me. And I do want to fit in with your plan for my life, so that I can serve you as you want me to. Amen.

THE SAME MESSAGE

It was Thanksgiving today, God. We heard the same thing we hear every year: "God is good—give thanks." It's like that at Christmas. Every Christmas Eve, every Christmas Day, we hear again: "For to you is born this day in the city of David a Savior, who is Christ the Lord." And we know now what we're going to hear on Easter: "Christ is risen!" We've heard it all before. And before. And before.

But that's just what I want to thank you for, God. Thank you that we are able to hear the same messages year in and year out, because there's blessing in truth that, by its very nature, remains unchanged. And there's blessing in my hearing that truth again and again.

That's not at all surprising, is it, seeing that these truths come from you? Amen.

Bless our home

Dear Lord, thank you for both our house and our home.

When my husband gave up his last job we had to move here to a much smaller house, leaving some comforts behind. But it hasn't mattered. We've been just as happy, if not happier, here in our new house.

I guess that shows that we can make a home anywhere. It's also taught me that a home can be happy and secure when it has you at its center, wherever that home may be housed.

Be present always in this house to bless the home that is here. And when our children leave to go to different houses to establish new homes, again, bless also those houses and homes with your presence.

May our homes be, in a small way, forerunners of that perfect home we will share one day with you when we'll be living in the mansions that you have promised us. Amen.

Your LOVE FOR ME

Dear God, I can't help thinking that you see me as I see my tatty old cardigan. It's old and it's out of shape, but it's one of my favorite pieces of clothing. It's so comfortable and warm that I just can't bring myself to throw it away.

I'm old and out of shape, but you're not going to discard me either. You've declared in more ways than one that I'm very precious to you. Thank you, God, that no matter how much older I get, how much more misshapen or wrinkled or decrepit I may become, your love for me will never waver: you'll never desert me or reject me. At my weakest times your love is there for me in all its strength. And always will be.

I praise such love and I rest in it, knowing it will take me through into an eternity with you. Amen.

ACCEPTING EVERYONE

Dear Lord, I'd never call myself a snob. And yet, when I probe really deep inside myself, I see traces of judgment and rejection toward some of the down-and-outs in my area.

Some might say that's not being snobbish; that's simply sizing up a situation. Whether that's so or not, what I do know and what I can't escape from is that your love was and is for everyone and that it's unconditional. Surely then, since I'm your disciple, my love has to follow the same pattern and simply *be* there for people, regardless of their background and their situation.

Forgive my quickness to condemn certain people and to dismiss them with no further thought for their welfare. And give me instead a spirit of openness and acceptance that is prepared to help anyone in need. Surely that's what I would want for myself from others. Amen.

TEACH ME FORGIVENESS

Dear God, you know about this thing that's happened between my husband and me. It wasn't such a big thing really, yet I'm so upset over it. He's done the same thing before. He said then he was sorry, but now he goes and does it all over again! As your child I know what I'm supposed to do: forgive him. But how can I forgive when the hurt is so deep?

"As far as the east is from the west, so far he removes our transgressions from us" (Psalm 103:12). Is it merely coincidence that this was part of our Bible reading this evening? Dear God, it must hurt you every time I sin—every time I violate your perfection with my wrongdoing. And yet you forgive me. Over and over again.

I still don't feel like forgiving my husband. But since I know how your ready forgiveness of me has brought healing into my life (and it's healing that we need now), I do want *to forgive him. Empower me now by your Holy Spirit to do just that. Amen.*

Make me like Jesus

Holy Spirit, I ask that you make me the sort of person in whom others can see Jesus. You'll have a job and a half on your hands to do this. No one knows that better than I (apart from you, that is).

But I'm simply asking that your mighty power—your almighty power—keep on working in me to make me more and more like Jesus. I guess most of the time I won't even be aware of your makeover job on me. That doesn't matter. As long as others see the Jesus-like qualities you are producing in me: humility, kindness, patience, gentleness, and whatever else you desire—and are blessed by them. I know it will be a long haul, but I'm trusting you, Spirit of God, to do your work within me.

I admire your persistence and I praise your power. Amen.

A TIRED MOTHER

O God, please make the baby sleep for a couple of hours! I'm so tired, I feel sick. I had no idea that looking after a baby would be so wearying and so demanding. And so *constant:* there's always something that has to be done.

I'm very glad that, as my heavenly Lord, you never get tired of looking after me. Look after me now at this busy time. Give me the strength I need to do the things that have to be done, and the sense to let go of those things that can wait.

And thank you for this precious bundle that is turning our lives upside down. Amen.

GOD'S GOODNESS

God, thank you for all these pears—windfalls though they be—that I am peeling and slicing, each little greeny-yellow fruit a tangible sign of your goodness toward us as you provide for us.

And then, as I pause to look up and out through the glass doors, I thank you also for the gladdening spirit of a fully opened giant red hibiscus bloom proclaiming your glory to the potted orchid beside it, and to the cat sheltering beneath it.

Your love for us is set before us wherever we turn. Give us the eyes, the heart, and the mind to see it. Amen.

A GOSSIP SESSION

Dear God, I wonder what you thought of our little gossip session today? We didn't say anything really bad about anyone, did we? It was more a case of stating facts as we saw them, wasn't it?

Then why do I feel uneasy about it all? Is it because, deep down, I know that, in your eyes, my faults are just as bad as the faults of those people we threw around in our conversation today?

I guess I'll never really learn as I should that what I see as "little" sins in myself are just as bad as what I see as "bigger" sins in others. That attitude is, in itself, a sin for which I need to ask your forgiveness.

Help me more and more to recognize and confess the sin that is within me. *Thank you for the full forgiveness that is always there for me in Jesus—and that is there for others too. Amen.*

A SINGLE MOTHER

I've been noticing, God, that there are more and more of us single mothers around. Perhaps that's why people don't look askance at me as much as they used to. It's true that, as a single mom, I'm generally accepted in society.

But that doesn't make my job any easier. Even though I have the support of my parents and my friends, it's still finally my responsibility to provide a home and a good up-bringing for my daughter.

This is where I'm so thankful, God, that both she and I have a Dad in you. We need your fatherly protection, guidance, and strength. Thank you that on my really down days—those days when I feel my aloneness so keenly—I can know that you're still there for me, even though you may seem far away.

Work things out well in both my life and hers. I know I can trust you to do this, because you love us both very much. Amen.

THE COMPANY OF OTHERS

Lord, there's a big hole in our lives now that our friends have left. What good times we had together! Even when things were bad, our times together were good.

I guess, in your whole plan of things, it's now time for others to enjoy their company and to benefit from all that they have to give.

It looks as though there's a lesson for me to learn in all of this: the lesson that I never begrudge the loss of someone or something that has blessed me, when that person or thing can bless others elsewhere. I don't like this lesson, Lord—it's a hard one. But, with your help, I believe I can learn it. Amen.

THANKS FOR YOUR CARE

I can hardly believe, Lord, how, after all my concern, things have gone so well for my son. He found accommodation so quickly. And look at the way his travel arrangements for his work study worked out so well! All the pieces of the jigsaw puzzle have come together.

But then you always do put the puzzle pieces of our lives together. How could I ever have doubted that you would do it for him? Forgive me. And thank you.

As you've shown me yet again your faithfulness in caring for your children, so increase my confidence in you to look after him for the rest of the year—especially when things are not going so well for him. Amen.

Our church family

I've been so blessed again today, Lord, just by being with my church family. They're so thoughtful, loving, and caring.

I've gathered that not all church families are like this. I don't know why it is that ours is blessed in this way while others struggle to find harmony and a sharing of love and concern.

Lord Jesus, I pray for your whole church on earth: for all who confess you as Savior and Lord. Give us all a greater love for you, so that we will love each other more. And then, as a people united in our love for you and for one another, make us your front line of loving, caring action in a world that so often knows no love at all.

May your Spirit—the very Spirit of love—bring all this about. Amen.

CONCERN FOR OTHERS

Lord, I needed that cuppa! Very hot, not too strong, six drops of milk—just the way I like it.

I *am* blessed with my home comforts: food to be had any time of the day or night; a bed that's just right for my weary bones; tea when I want it. Not like some.

I need a lot of reminding, Lord, that most people in the world can't get a drink of clean water, let alone a cup of tea. Forgive my regular forgetfulness of this fact—and my apathy when I do remember it. Give me a concern for those who suffer the stress and the indignity—and the sheer waste—of doing nothing day after day but struggling to stay alive. And then, as further evidence of your love within me, turn my concern into action. Amen.

WEDDING ANNIVERSARY

It's our wedding anniversary, Lord. Where *have* the years gone?

I'm very grateful for my husband's love and care and faithfulness all these past years. I'm also grateful, Lord, for your faithfulness toward us in our marriage. We've been through some pretty tough times, and you've always been there with us. Not only have you helped us out of some tight corners, but you've been with us also on our good days, protecting us, guiding us, and, above all, keeping us close to you and to each other.

Just as the relationship we have with each other is precious to us, so is the relationship we have with you. I pray, dear God, that both relationships will last—the latter one taking us right through into eternity. Amen.

A SCRIPTURE LESSON

Well, that's another Scripture lesson I've survived, Lord. Just. The children were particularly restless today. I wonder if anything at all got through to them. Maybe doing all that blackboard work wasn't the right way to go. Maybe my pictures weren't big enough.

When I think about it all a bit more, I'm so glad, Holy Spirit, that you were in that classroom with me. That means that the message *was* getting through to someone because, after all, you're the one who does the real work at these times—and you're the power of God Almighty!

I praise your power, and thank you that you go to work wherever and whenever God's word is spoken. You'll bring blessing to the children in that classroom in spite of all my mistakes and deficiencies.

Thanks for reminding me of this today. I'll take any encouragement I can get. Amen.

Children Leaving Home

Lord, I'm feeling more than a bit low since it's hitting home that my children really are grown up and are capable of standing on their own two feet. I know it's normal and right and good that they are leaving home—this home—to make their own homes. But that doesn't take away that big of emptiness inside me—even loneliness—and a longing for their company.

I know you can identify with me because you had a much worse time of it when you were separated from your Son as he hung on the cross. You and he were even closer to one another than I am to my children. As I look at the cross I see also how you were prepared to let go of your Son. Help me now to let go of my children.

Because you understand my situation so well, I'm sure you'll do something to compensate for my feeling of aloneness. After all, it was because of your love for me that you went through that painful time of being apart from Jesus. Thank you for your love for me then, and for your love that I'll be experiencing in the days ahead. Amen.

WAITING FOR BABY'S BIRTH

Thank you, Lord, for the miracle of life I am carrying within me. You created this baby, and so there's already something very wonderful about him.

I hand this child over to you because I want your blessing on him throughout his life—starting now. Bless his development within my womb, and please give us a healthy baby. I'm looking forward to his becoming your child in baptism; the best thing he could have in his life is a lasting relationship with you.

Thank you that my hsuband's and my love for each other has been able to find tangible expression in this new life. And thank you for the excitement we can share as we await our baby's birth. Amen.

THANKS FOR GOD'S ACCEPTANCE

I want to thank you, Lord, that because of Jesus I can, as your child, bask in your parental approval. In this approval, you give me the freedom to be myself—to be to the fullest the person you have always intended me to be. It's good to know this when others, in some way, let me know that I don't fit into the mold they think I should.

Help me, though, not to be insensitive toward other people's outlooks; and, especially, help me not to ignore whatever you have to say to me in your word.

May my freedom in Jesus never become an excuse for doing whatever I like. Rather, let it be the means by which my life can more and more give glory to you. Amen.

PRAYER IN CRISIS

It's crisis time all right, isn't it, God? You ought to know after all the prayers that have been coming your way. Of course, all along you've known all the intricacies of this messy, difficult situation better than we have; even though my friend and I have spent hours talking everything through.

And what a comfort that is! Having brought to you our specific requests, we can now relax (please help us to!) in the confidence that you have the whole thing in hand. In fact, I'm quite excited to see what you're going to do for her! She's had her problems in the past, and you've never let her down. No doubt, you'll see her through this crisis too.

We're trusting you, Lord. Increase our trust in you as we wait for you to act. Amen.

A SICK CHILD

Dear Lord Jesus, my little girl is so sick and I feel so helpless. When she wakes now and then from her fitful sleep, there's nothing I can do to ease her distress. All I can do is wait and hope for an improvement—and talk to you.

Place your healing hand on her, Jesus, and make her better. In your love for her, and with your mighty power, ease her pain and bring her back to full health.

I praise your greatness that is perfect in its goodness toward her. Because she belongs to God through your death and resurrection, nothing can really hurt her at this time; and I thank you for that.

Please, Jesus, turn my distress into delight for the sake of your love for both her and me. Amen.

WHILE FISHING

Lord, this fishing is more fun than I thought it would be! The thrill of feeling a tug at the end of the line and reeling in a fish hasn't happened very often. But there's so much else to enjoy as I stand at the water's edge.

Each wave, as it rises, becomes a stretch of clear green glass through which I can see the pebbles on the sea bed. And then, as it rolls over and creams and froths its way toward me, we play together the game of touch and run. The seagulls are showing off their poise and speed as they dive-bomb unsuspecting fish further out to sea; while further out still, the line of the horizon bumps and jumps with the movement of the mass of water beneath it.

The beauty and wonder of it all are enough to compensate for wet feet and chilled hands. And cause to praise you, the Creator and Lord of the sea, the gulls, and the fish. Amen.

PRAYER FOR PROTECTION

Dear Lord, we all need your protection. My husband needs it as he drives to work; I need it in and around the home (don't they say most accidents occur in the home?); and the children need it as they go through their school day. We need physical protection, but we also need protection from anything that can harm us emotionally or spiritually.

You're the one with the power to protect us from everything that is harmful. In Jesus' death and resurrection we have seen you as the great Protector, the one who is able to protect us from the terrible consequences of sin.

Thank you for the confidence this gives me to hand over into your capable hands myself and my loved ones for this day. Amen.

I'VE FAILED AGAIN

Lord, I've messed up again. There were people relying on me, and I forgot to do what I was supposed to do.

I feel awful. For a start, my pride is hurt (what will they think of me?). And then, I've put these people out; someone's now got to make up for my ineptitude.

I'm starting to feel better, though, for having unburdened this onto you. In fact, I'm not nearly so worried now about the repercussions of my action—or, rather, my inaction; because I'm going to leave this latest mess in your hands, seeing I can do no more about it at this stage. Thank you for being so understanding and helpful.

P.S. Thanks especially that you still love me in spite of my blunders.

P.P.S. Please help me be a bit more on the ball in the future! Amen.

Monday morning blues

Ugh! Whoever first coined that phrase "Monday morning blues," Lord, was right on the money. I know I shouldn't think of my work as drudgery, but it's been awfully hard getting myself off to work this morning.

I guess, Jesus, that your work routine when you were on earth wasn't a bundle of excitement for you either. You did the same hard work day after day: hours of preaching, teaching, and healing, made all the more difficult by almost constant opposition. And then, at the end of the day, you didn't even have a place to call your own and in which to relax.

In light of all that, it seems that the least I can do is keep on giving my job my best shot until you might want me somewhere else. Help me with my work. And put a song in my heart on Monday mornings—especially on Monday mornings—just because I'm your child and you love me. Amen.

At a crossroads

Lord, I'm at a crossroads in my life and it doesn't feel good. I don't know which road I'm meant to take. I don't even know where the roads lead to.

My role in life has, up till now, been pretty clear-cut. When I was first married, I had my full-time job; and then, as the children came, I worked full-time at home. More lately, I've had my part-time job. But now, with all the children having left home, and hardly anything for me to do in the house, my part-time job isn't satisfying enough.

I can't go back to my old full-time job: younger, more qualified people are lining up for that these days.

Please come and sit with me at my crossroads, Lord; and then point me in the direction that you have in mind for me to follow. I know that I can trust you to direct my life now, just as you have in the past. Help me to be patient as I wait for your perfect timing in opening and shutting doors for me. Amen.

A SPECIAL OUTFIT

God, I'm tired! But I must finish this shopping. And I still must decide today on an outfit for the wedding.

There's that gorgeous outfit I saw: that two-piece in that beautiful soft fabric in vibrant midnight blue. It looked great when I tried it on, and blue *is* my color. But it costs the earth. Still, this is a rather special occasion.

I'm so glad, God, that I don't have to worry about what outfit to wear for that extra special occasion in my life: the day when I'll be meeting you face to face. You yourself will have given it to me. And what a stunner I'll look, dressed in the gown of Jesus' righteousness! Any compliments I may get at the wedding will be nothing compared with your approval of me on that day.

Thank you, God, for giving me this marvelous outfit. I know it cost you heaps. Help me to value it and prize it above everything else. Even above gorgeous, vibrant, midnight blue two-pieces. Amen.

Help me to love

God, I want you to perform a little miracle for me. Well—it may have to be a fairly big one. I need you to give me a love for my friend.

You know how irritating she is. How gossipy. And how she goes on and on. And yet I know that it's just not right for me to be avoiding her and to have this negative feeling toward her; because I know you love her deeply. So much so that you let your Son die for her. If *you* love her, how can I *not* love her?

Holy Spirit, give me the love of God so that I can love her. Give me a love for her that sees past her failings to the real person inside who is made in God's image and is precious to God. After all, that's how God looks at me. And if we're going to start talking about personal faults—well, I'd rather we didn't.

So there you are, God of miracles. Please work a miracle for me. Amen.

PATIENCE TO BE A GOOD MOM

Dear Lord, I'm beginning to see all my that my mother went through in raising us children. I've just had my fourth—and probably not my last—sleepless night this week. If I can muster the energy, I must call Mom and thank her. Or I might send her some flowers with a short note. She'd like that.

I'm seeing for myself, Lord, how being a mom can be such hard work. I really want to do a good job of bringing up my children, but the energy and patience wear pretty thin at times.

What I need and what I'd love you to give me is patience, wisdom, strength, understanding—you know—the bringing-up-kids package: the one with the lot. I can assure you it won't go astray.

Because I know I can bank on your constant help, I'm trusting that both the children and I will come through the wear and tear OK. Help me believe it; especially when the 8:00 A.M. rush hour and the 5:00 P.M. tantrums would indicate otherwise. Amen.

ANOTHER YEAR OLDER

Well, that's another birthday come and gone, God; another year that's brought a few more gray hairs and a further deterioration in eyesight.

But maybe it's not all bad, growing one year older. That's another year that the Spirit has had in which to work on me, in which to bring me closer to you and to make me more like Jesus. So, in growing older, maybe I've gained some good things too. In fact, with your power at work for me, I'd have to believe that I'm now one year better off. Through your word, your Spirit must have brought home to me some new spiritual truths this past year. And, when I think of that bad stretch I went through, I remember how the Spirit deepened my relationship with you by opening my eyes to see the greatness of your love and faithfulness toward your child in need. Perhaps your Spirit has also given me a more compassionate, less judgmental attitude toward others, and perhaps pried me a little further from my self-centeredness, so that I'm freer to be concerned about others and to be more active in helping them. I hope so. And may the Spirit keep on working on me in this new year of my life. Amen.

God works for good

Dear Lord, I'm overawed as I think about the good that came about through my friend's dying. How we prayed for her physical healing! But now she is with you in a far better world, and we who knew her are all the richer because of her manner of dying.

In those last months and especially in those last days, all of us who spent time with her were blessed by the strength of her faith in you as her Savior, and by her joy in the fact that she was about to begin a wonderful new life with you. She was so eager to speak about you, and about your love—not only for her, but for all people.

I pray that the impact made on the rest of us by her confident dying will help strengthen us in our faith for a long time to come. Also that, encouraged by her example, we will become bolder in sharing the gospel message with others.

Here, Lord, was yet another example of how you are able to bring good out of what at first appears to be only bad. I praise such power. Amen.

Make me a true friend

Save me, Lord, from being a fair-weather friend: one who enjoys my friends' company while things go well for them, but ignores them when they come up against difficulties in their lives. Grant that I can be a blessing to my friends *especially* when they are going through a hard time.

At such times give me ears and eyes that listen and see with understanding, as well as compassion. And then, to my understanding and compassion, add sensitivity, so that whatever I do for my friends will truly be helpful.

Thank you for my friends and all the good things they bring into my life. Make me, Lord, a true friend to them. Amen.

BLESS THAT HURTING WOMAN

Lord, I needed to drop in at the medical center today. As I waited at the desk, I glanced around at the people sitting in the sun-flooded waiting room.

In one corner sat a middle-aged woman. She was looking away from the others, her body hunched up in itself, her eyes red and swollen from weeping. She was obviously struggling to keep her emotions under control. In her hurt, this beautiful day of winter sunshine would have meant little, if anything, to her.

Lord, be with this woman and bless her, giving her whatever she needs at this time. Shine on her, Jesus, with the full warmth of your love, so that good things will be included in whatever lies ahead for her. Thank you. Amen.

For all people

So often, Jesus, my prayers center on me and my little world. Expand my vision so that I also more regularly pray:

for countries torn apart by war;
for those who suffer from natural disasters;
for the victims of injustice and oppression;
for my country and its leaders;
for the leaders of all countries;

and for all who, in their faith, love, and obedience toward you, and by the power of the Holy Spirit, are, in some way, carrying on with the work you began here on earth. Amen.

Bless My Grandchildren

God, thank you for these precious little beings—my grandchildren. I love their fresh, eager, smiling faces; and their little serious frowns when they have to grapple with something that must be learned in this big, complex world.

I'm sure I'm praying more for my grandchildren than I ever did for my own children. I guess that's one of the special privileges and joys of us grandmas: we're far enough removed from the constant demands of child-raising, first of all to have time to think about praying, and second, to actually do it.

Bless them, Lord, these children who are so precious to you as well as to me. Bless their total development. And grant that, above all, they will love you and serve you their whole lives. Amen.

A CREATIVE GOD

It was fun to have this special meal tonight, Lord. I enjoyed planning the menu and working out how I could do things a little differently here, or add a special touch there. And it was fun thinking up a new table setting.

I enjoyed the chance to be creative. When I think about it, it seems to me that the wonderful thing about creativity is that there's no end to its possibilities; when you begin on a creative task, you never really know what the final outcome will be, do you?

I'm very glad that I belong to a creative God. There's nothing static or dull about you. Your vibrancy and the depth and breadth of you is all around me in your created world. What's more, your creativity comes right into my life, creating new settings and new opportunities for me, which in turn provide me with new interests, new activities, and new joys. I even carry your creative presence within me in the person of your Spirit. Since he was able to carry out that mighty act of re-creation at my baptism, who knows what he might achieve within me and through me now? Amen.

Out of control

Lord, I'm frightened. Everything is moving out of my control, and I have this sick feeling that I'm just not going to make it.

I know you love me and that you are in control of my life, and that all things work together for good to those who love you. But I still feel awful.

Help me. Above all, give me your Holy Spirit to give me your peace—peace to drive out my fears and to calm and quiet my whole being.

Grant that, in the future, I'll be able to look back on this period of my life and see how wonderfully you were there for me all the time. Until then, keep your Holy Spirit with me to be my comforter, my guide, and my strength. May the Spirit also increase my trust in you—a trust that you are hard at work right now to help me.

Thank you, Lord, for your care of me at this time. Amen.

Thanks for My Children

Lord, when I see a maturity in my children, a wisdom in the way they think and act, all I can do is thank you from the bottom of my heart and praise your grace. Because it's only through your goodness that my children have turned out so well.

You and I know what a poor mother I was at times. You know my heartache when I recall some of the things I said and did as a mom, and the things I didn't do and say. And yet here are these fine young adults. Which all goes to show the power and healing that lie in your forgiveness. As we turn to you in our messes, you can turn things around for us.

I pray that you continue to heal any harm that came to my children because of me. And I pray that they too will know, one day, when they make their parenting mistakes, that your love for them and their children is great enough to forgive the wrong and to heal it. Amen.

POTENTIAL FOR NEW GROWTH

Lord, I felt a bit depressed after my friend's visit today. She hadn't seen my garden since the height of summer, when it was looking so lush and alive. Her remark, "There's not much in it," was understandable. The garden is sparse and very lackluster now in winter, not only because most of it is having its necessary rest, but also because I remodeled a whole section of it late last summer. Those plants are very young and still have a lot of growing to do, which will come only in the warmer months.

You know, Lord, how I sometimes feel thin and lackluster inside. Remind me then that I still, at such times, carry within me the fullness and richness of your Spirit—just as my bare-looking garden at the moment is loaded with life, albeit hidden. And help me remember that it's precisely because of the bleakness of my cold bare days, and therefore my greater dependency on you, that the Spirit is able to bring about growth and resulting lushness in my spiritual life. Amen.

The beauty of nature

Lord, it was good today to visit a pocket of your world where nature has remained relatively untouched by humans. We saw an abundance of unfamiliar plant life and bird life. The area rang with the clear calls of the birds. We observed animals a short distance from us; and the various scents gave a pungency to the crisp clear air.

Yes, it was good to be there, Lord. Forgive us for where we've shown disregard for the world of nature and, in so doing, have insulted you, its planner and creator—and have also contributed toward the current ecological situation that is proving harmful to us.

Give us the heart and the wisdom to care for your created world as we should. By your grace, may we be able to correct much of the damage that has been done. Help me play my part in this, small though it may be. Amen.

Money worries

God, you know how uptight I get at times about our financial situation. The bills keep coming in. And then, just when we think we're getting our head above water, something extra crops up, like repairs to the house or a trip to the dentist. It's hard not to worry about whether or not we'll have the money when we need it.

Then I think of how you provided for the children of Israel in the desert, and for the thousands of people who stayed so long listening to Jesus that they got hungry. You're the same God today. You're still looking after people—still providing them with what they need, both materially and spiritually.

Save me, Lord, from envy of others who appear to be better off than we are. We are rich in having you as our God: all the riches of your love for us in Jesus are ours for the asking and the taking! Thank you for making us so wealthy.

Remind me often of your love for us. Help me manage my money carefully and wisely. And give me peace as I trust you to care for us. Amen.

OUT OF WORK

Lord, I don't have a job, but at least I have you. Without you, I think my self-esteem would be at rock bottom; it's not at all nice to be made to feel so useless. But I know *you* don't see me as useless; you made me with gifts and abilities with which I can bless others. If I can't do that these days through a work situation, then show me other ways in which I can.

I know also that I'm important enough to you for you to have mapped out a plan for my life. I want to trust you to lead me now according to that plan, whether it will be to a job or into some other worthwhile avenue. Trusting becomes a bit hard when nothing seems to be happening. Help me hang in there with you and believe that you are *arranging things for my welfare. Amen.*

CELEBRATING TOGETHER

Thank you, Lord, that the whole family can be together this Christmas. Thank you for our children and our grandchildren, and for all the happiness we can experience with one another as we celebrate this holy season.

Please grant, Lord, that your Spirit keep alive in each one of us the faith in Jesus that we share, so that we will be together again one day in that greatest of all celebrations when we gather around your throne in heaven.

These are wonderful days that we are having together, but they're not perfect. The youngest needed a lot of pacifying this afternoon when she got a splinter; and parents' tempers were a little frayed after that recent shopping excursion (which also gave me an aching back). But our next life with you will *be perfect! It's marvelous—something truly to be marveled at—that there's something still to come that's even better than these good days we are enjoying now. And for that also I thank you and praise you. Amen.*